This Bucket List Journal Belongs To:

_____

My Bucket List

Bucket List

What

Why _____   How _____

_____   _____

_____   _____

_____   _____

Completed

Date _____   Where _____

With _____

Notes/Thoughts/Memories

_____

_____

_____

_____

_____

Would I Do It Again?   yes ☐   no ☐

Memories In Pictures

Souvenirs

Bucket List

What

Why _____   How _____

_____   _____

_____   _____

_____   _____

Completed

Date _____   Where _____

With _____

Notes/Thoughts/Memories

_____

_____

_____

_____

_____

_____

Would I Do It Again?   yes ☐   no ☐

Memories In Pictures

Souvenirs

Bucket List

What

Why _____   How _____

_____   _____

_____   _____

_____   _____

Completed

Date _____   Where _____

With _____

Notes/Thoughts/Memories

_____

_____

_____

_____

_____

_____

_____

Would I Do It Again?   yes ☐   no ☐

Memories In Pictures

Souvenirs

Bucket List

What

Why _____

_____

_____

_____

How _____

_____

_____

_____

Completed

Date _____

Where _____

With _____

Notes/Thoughts/Memories

_____

_____

_____

_____

_____

_____

Would I Do It Again?

yes ☐

no ☐

Memories In Pictures

Souvenirs

Bucket List

What

Why _____

_____

_____

_____

How _____

_____

_____

_____

Completed

Date _____   Where _____

With _____

Notes/Thoughts/Memories

_____

_____

_____

_____

_____

_____

_____

Would I Do It Again?   yes ☐   no ☐

Memories In Pictures

Souvenirs

Bucket List

What

Why _____

How _____

_____

_____

_____

_____

_____

Completed

Date _____

Where _____

With _____

Notes/Thoughts/Memories

_____

_____

_____

_____

_____

_____

Would I Do It Again?

yes ☐   no ☐

Memories In Pictures

Souvenirs

Bucket List

What

Why _____   How _____

_____   _____

_____   _____

_____   _____

Completed

Date _____   Where _____

With _____

Notes/Thoughts/Memories

_____

_____

_____

_____

_____

_____

                              yes   no
Would I Do It Again?   ☐   ☐

Memories In Pictures

Souvenirs

Bucket List

What

Why _____

_____

_____

_____

How _____

_____

_____

_____

Completed

Date _____

Where _____

With _____

Notes/Thoughts/Memories

_____

_____

_____

_____

_____

_____

_____

Would I Do It Again?   yes ☐   no ☐

Memories In Pictures

Souvenirs

Bucket List

What

Why _____

How _____

_____

_____

_____

_____

_____

Completed

Date _____

Where _____

With _____

Notes/Thoughts/Memories

_____

_____

_____

_____

_____

_____

_____

Would I Do It Again?   yes ☐   no ☐

Memories In Pictures

Souvenirs

Bucket List

What

Why _____

_____

_____

_____

How _____

_____

_____

Completed

Date _____

Where _____

With _____

Notes/Thoughts/Memories

_____

_____

_____

_____

_____

_____

Would I Do It Again?   yes ☐   no ☐

Memories In Pictures

Souvenirs

Bucket List

What

Why _____

How _____

_____

_____

_____

_____

_____

_____

Completed

Date _____

Where _____

With _____

Notes/Thoughts/Memories

_____

_____

_____

_____

_____

_____

Would I Do It Again?   yes ☐   no ☐

Memories In Pictures

Souvenirs

Bucket List

What

Why _____   How _____

_____   _____

_____   _____

_____

Completed

Date _____   Where _____

With _____

Notes/Thoughts/Memories

_____

_____

_____

_____

_____

_____

Would I Do It Again?   yes ☐   no ☐

Memories In Pictures

Souvenirs

Bucket List

What

Why

How

Completed

Date

Where

With

Notes/Thoughts/Memories

Would I Do It Again?   yes ☐   no ☐

Memories In Pictures

Souvenirs

Bucket List

What

Why _____

_____

_____

_____

How _____

_____

_____

Completed

Date _____

Where _____

With _____

Notes/Thoughts/Memories

_____

_____

_____

_____

_____

_____

Would I Do It Again?   yes ▢   no ▢

Memories In Pictures

Souvenirs

Bucket List

What

Why _____   How _____

_____   _____

_____   _____

_____

Completed

Date _____   Where _____

With _____

Notes/Thoughts/Memories

_____

_____

_____

_____

_____

_____

_____

yes   no
Would I Do It Again?   ☐   ☐

Memories In Pictures

Souvenirs

Bucket List

What

Why _____

How _____

_____

_____

_____

_____

Completed

Date _____

Where _____

With _____

Notes/Thoughts/Memories

_____

_____

_____

_____

_____

Would I Do It Again?   yes ☐   no ☐

Memories In Pictures

Souvenirs

Bucket List

What

Why _____   How _____

_____   _____

_____   _____

_____   _____

Completed

Date _____   Where _____

With _____

Notes/Thoughts/Memories

_____

_____

_____

_____

_____

_____

_____

Would I Do It Again?   yes ☐   no ☐

Memories In Pictures

Souvenirs

Bucket List

What

Why _____   How _____

_____   _____

_____   _____

_____   _____

Completed

Date _____   Where _____

With _____

Notes/Thoughts/Memories

_____

_____

_____

_____

_____

Would I Do It Again?   yes ☐   no ☐

Memories In Pictures

Souvenirs

Bucket List

What

Why _____

How _____

_____

_____

_____

_____

_____

Completed

Date _____

Where _____

With _____

Notes/Thoughts/Memories

_____

_____

_____

_____

_____

_____

Would I Do It Again?

yes ☐   no ☐

Memories In Pictures

Souvenirs

Journal

Journal

Journal

Journal

Journal

Journal

Journal

Journal

Journal

Journal

Journal

Journal

Journal

Journal

Journal

Journal

Journal

Journal

Journal

Journal

Journal

Journal

Journal

Journal

Journal

Journal

Journal

_____

_____

_____

_____

_____

_____

_____

_____

_____

_____

_____

_____

_____

_____

_____

_____

_____

_____

_____

_____

Journal

Journal

Journal

Journal

Made in the USA
Monee, IL
14 November 2020